EPSOM

TO E
From EW.

-6 MAY 2000
16.5.2000

14 DEC 2000

56 JAN 200
5 FEB 2001

19 MAR 2001

3 0 JUN 2001

-2 AUG 2001

1 SEP 01

29 AUG 2002 E.P

4 OCT 02

TO: RUE
FROM: EP

BL

LASER
TO. DENMARK.
FR. EPSOM SY.
DIB 22/4/03.
APP 6630026/
HT

-8 NOV 2003

TO. E.P
FROM. RJE

A ♀ Sparrowhawk quarters low over the fields scattering small groups of lapwings & Golden Plover

Towards the Sea

Robert Greenhalf
Towards the Sea

Pica
PRESS

PICA PRESS

SUSSEX

For Mum, Sally and Jack,
and to the memory of Dad

© 1999 Robert Greenhalf

Pica Press
(an imprint of Helm Information Ltd.)
The Banks, Mountfield,
Nr. Robertsbridge,
East Sussex TN32 5JY

ISBN 1-873403-89-5

A catalogue record for this book is available from the British Library.

Editor: Nigel Redman
Designer: Julie Reynolds

Production and design by Fluke Art, Bexhill on Sea, E Sussex
Printed in Italy by Giunti Industrie Grafiche

Acknowledgements

Writing and painting are essentially solitary occupations, yet without the help and support of many friends and my family this book could not have materialised.

I would like to thank everyone who has helped in various ways by providing me with good company, transport, hospitality, information, advice, ideas, encouragement, access to land, or just good old 'tea and sympathy', especially: Kim Atkinson and Gwydion Morley, Mary and Pat Bonham, Vanessa Hedley, Ysbrand Brouwers of Artists for Nature Foundation, Andrew and Megan Haslen and Graham Barker of the Wildlife Art Gallery in Lavenham, Christopher and Deborah Harrison of Bircham Contemporary Arts in Holt, Eric Money of Rye Art Gallery, Philip Merricks, Stephen Rumsey and John Willsher, Matthew and Lizzie Thomas, Barry and Anne Yates of Rye Harbour Nature Reserve.

I am greatly indebted to Christopher and Amanda Helm and Nigel Redman of Pica Press for having enough faith in, and enthusiasm for, my work to resurrect and publish this book. I have to thank Julie Reynolds of Fluke Art also, for so ably carrying out the vital job of assembling my text and pictures into a cohesive design, and seeing the whole project through the precarious production stages.

A number of the pictures in this book are in private collections, and I would like to thank the various owners for kindly agreeing to their reproduction here. A big thank you also to my brother Pete who photographed many of the paintings.

Finally and most importantly, love and thanks to my wife Sally and our son Jack for their support and encouragement; for putting up with my absences from home whilst I was working on the Norfolk and Bardsey chapters, and for Sally's reading, correcting and typing of the text.

Introduction

"It is low tide at Star Lock. The last thin silver ribbon of water snakes its way towards the sea. The river, held back by the lock gates, awaits the tide's return. There are young Shelducks feeding close to the lock – too close, they tolerate me as I walk slowly past, but when I stop they are off, taking with them every other bird on the stretch: off go the Redshanks and Greenshanks, sending a frenzy of alarm calls ringing from the mud banks, spreading panic to the Herring Gulls and a solitary Grey Heron that lifts off heavily and heads downstream. But I needn't have worried; by the time my telescope is on its tripod, and paper, pencils and paints are ready, the Shelducks are back, circling low before making slightly undignified landings on the wet mud. Before long the Redshanks and Greenshanks also return. Wary at first, they become reconciled to my intrusion and are soon feeding again.

With barely two hours before the light goes, speed is essential. I work with a pencil at first, drawing in the bones of the composition – the bold rounded shapes of mud banks that spring from the meandering loops of the stream. Birds are incorporated to counter-balance, complement, or contrast, to add life and movement to the scene. The light is perfect now, low in the sky, a little to the right; it bounces a warm glow from the wet mud and the white flanks of the Shelducks and gulls. Shadows are of the most delicate purple-blue. Mud, water and birds are as one, mirrors of the sky, each facet reflecting a different colour, each changing with the light. Frantically I wash in colours, trying to record as much as I can before the light changes. The watercolour dries very slowly in the damp evening air. I struggle towards the result I want, blotting here, adding more colour there, but you are never completely in control of watercolour, especially not at this time of day."

This extract from my diary for 1st September gave me both the title to this book and a fitting introduction, describing as it does the pleasures and the problems of working 'in the field' direct from nature. Each page is my record of a day, or sometimes just an hour or two, spent observing, drawing and painting from life. Together they record some of my experiences of painting wildlife in the landscape throughout the year. The finished watercolours were also painted in the field with the subject before me. I find that working in this way forces me to be quick and intuitive, resulting in a more lively, spontaneous and convincing picture than I can usually achieve in the studio. The atmosphere directly influences the painting and becomes a part of it in an altogether appropriate way, for on a hot dry day the paint dries quickly: colours and outlines are crisp and sharp. In the damp evening air the paint barely dries at all, colours blend and outlines blur. There are many problems and many failures inherent in working in this way, but the feeling of elation I get when artist, paper, paint, water and weather have combined successfully, and I return home with a 'winner', is reward enough.

Home for me is Romney House. Built as a golf club house in the mid 1920s, it has the appearance of a colonial bungalow with a large veranda – its greatest asset. Perched on an ancient cliff line, we look out over Romney Marsh, south to Rye, east to Dungeness, and north-east to the distant North Downs where they meet the English Channel near Folkestone. Our garden, once laid out with trees, shrubs, hedges and lawn, had long been neglected when we moved here eight years ago. My wife, Sally, has made inroads into the sea of brambles, creating attractive borders to add colour and scent, but much of our three-quarters of an acre remains gloriously wild to support an impressive array of wildlife: dense thickets of shrubs and brambles provide nesting cover for Whitethroats, Lesser Whitethroats, Blackcaps, Willow Warblers, Linnets, Turtle Doves, Long-tailed Tits and Goldcrests, as well as the more usual garden species. There are mature ash, willow, apple and pear trees, and several statuesque *Cupressus* that tower to twice the height of the roof. A splendid storm-ravaged oak in the field just beyond our boundary provides food for tits and woodpeckers, and a refuge for noisy flocks of finches, sparrows, starlings and winter thrushes disturbed from the field. It is a vantage point for birds of prey and crows, and even a roost for Grey Herons.

From the sheltered confines of the garden we look out onto a very different landscape: below us, two fields distant, the River Rother wends its way to the sea some three miles to the south. Where once it would have sprawled across a wide estuary, it is now contained between banks, but the stretch as far as Star Lock is still tidal and the mudbanks exposed at low water provide rich feeding for Redshanks, Dunlins, Curlews, Shelducks and Grey Herons. With the rising tide in summer come fishing Common Terns, and autumn brings Greenshanks, Common Sandpipers, and a scattering of less common waders. Above the lock the river has been canalised and tamed, the home of Moorhens, Mallards and Kingfishers.

Beyond the river the eye roams freely over a huge acreage of sheep pasture and arable land, with little to stop it save the odd hawthorn break, occasional farmstead, marsh church, or distant village, each with their attendant shelter belt. The vast flatness of the marsh lies open to the skies, exposed to the full force of wind, rain and sun, unmoderated by hill or wood. On winter days especially, when the sun is low in the sky, even the smallest bush or bank can stand out as a prominent feature.

There has never been much need for hedges on the levels, for they are intersected by a network of dykes that both drain the land and retain the stock. Such hedges as do exist mainly border the winding marsh roads which often run along the old inning walls that claimed the land from the sea in centuries past. The marsh has many moods: bathed in hazy summer sun it can be soft and gentle; under winter storm clouds, bleak yet magnificent; or magical under a hoar frost, or when autumn mists leave only the tops of bushes exposed as islands in a sea of white. Always, the sky dominates. It is a landscape not easy to paint, its beauty transient and elusive, dependent upon atmosphere and light.

At the apex of the Romney Marsh triangle is Dungeness, strange and unique, a desert of shingle ridges thrown up by the sea. It is an important place for migrant birds and, a mile inland, the RSPB has created valuable gravel pit wetland habitats for nesting gulls, terns, ducks and waders, and wintering wildfowl. But for me the once unique atmosphere of the place is marred by the brooding presence of the two monstrous nuclear power stations. Like so many wild and wonderful places, Dungeness was written-off long ago as a wasteland, fit only it seems for army ranges and technological follies.

Fortunately, Rye Harbour Nature Reserve is in many ways like a miniature version of Dungeness. In May and June the shingle ridges which have looked bare throughout the winter months suddenly burst into life with colourful and unusual plants and nesting birds. The light is intense and dazzling at times. Agitated Little Terns rise to mob any birds foolish enough to cross their nesting ridges, Ringed Plovers, Oystercatchers and Wheatears share the shingle with them.

Ternery Pool, little more than a stone's throw from the sea, is the centre of activity throughout the year. A string of summer islands resound to the cries of breeding Common and Sandwich Terns, Black-headed Gulls, Redshanks and Ringed Plovers. At high tide they are joined by roosting waders. One of the islands is monopolised by Cormorants which come to bathe and rest. Strange, almost prehistoric, with wings outstretched, they are irresistible subjects to draw.

In the autumn and winter often large numbers of duck crowd in. From the two good hides overlooking Ternery Pool I can usually find a subject but, if not, there is another shallower and muddier pool created especially for waders where there are usually Redshanks, with snipe in winter and a variety of passage migrants in spring and autumn. Further inland are pools of a different nature. Some are large and deep with ducks and grebes, others are smaller, more secluded, fringed by lush reeds and with willow-clothed islands which, sometimes in winter, contain roosting Long-eared Owls and even the occasional Bittern.

West of Rye Harbour is Pett Level, the south-western corner of the marsh. Sheep and bullock-grazed pastures stretch back from the sea wall to the old cliff line below Winchelsea. In autumn and winter the damp pasture is an important feeding and high tide roosting area for many waders, most conspicuously several hundred Curlews. Long-billed and brown-chequered, they look splendid as they stalk amongst the sheep, often in the company of hyperactive flocks of starlings. There are pools here, too, where clay was dug out for the construction of the sea wall. They are shallow, with broad reed fringes in places that sometimes contain Bearded Tits and resound in summer to the clamour of Reed and Sedge Warblers. In July one of the pools adjacent to the coast road is drained by the Sussex Ornithological Society to provide a feeding area for passage waders. I often paint there, sitting on the sea wall so that I can also keep an eye on the beach. What at first sight appear to be rocks are, in fact, the remains of a centuries-old petrified forest, their peat-like nature and colour often disguised by a dark green weed. The incoming waves breaking against these 'rocks' make a dramatic backdrop to a composition of Oystercatchers or Curlews.

Although most of the marsh is well below sea level, modern pump drainage ensures that there are very few naturally wet areas left. However, in recent years two very important initiatives have been taken by conservation-minded landowners who, with the help of EEC grants, have recreated wetland areas that give some idea of what the lower-lying parts of the marsh would have been like a century or two ago.

In a valley that drains to the back of Pett Level, Stephen Rumsey, a keen birdwatcher and ringer, has created a superb area of pools and reedbeds which attract ducks and waders as well as large numbers of warblers, roosting Swallows and Sand Martins, and an impressive tally of rarities each year.

In a remote part of the marsh Philip Merricks, with the co-operation of several neighbouring farmers, floods a substantial area of low-lying ground each winter, with impressive results. I was privileged to be able to make a number of visits to this magnificent area to enjoy the spectacle of thousands of wildfowl and the often dramatic effects of light, wind and rain on this strange and lonely landscape of wide open horizons.

These are inspiring examples of what can be done to create wildlife habitat, encouraging exceptions to a general and continuing tide of habitat destruction.

This, then, is my home 'patch', a rich source of inspiration for much of my work. But from time to time I find it vital to have a change of scene, to provide the challenges and stimulation of the new and unfamiliar.

Bardsey Island proved to be ideal in every respect. Little more than a mile from end to end, it is a rock cast from the tip of the Lleyn Peninsula, the only tenuous link with the rest of Wales being a boat, if wind and tide permit. Here the sea dominates and controls, and you are never out of sight or sound of it.

There were unfamiliar subjects – Choughs, Ravens, Razorbills, Guillemots and Shags, alongside more familiar birds. But how different an Oystercatcher looks when viewed from the cliff-top above, as it probes amongst the swirling throngs of wrack and kelp. Bardsey is a place of passage, of comings and goings of both people and birds, their movements dictated by the weather – by the shipping forecast, not the traffic forecast.

On the face of it the North Norfolk coast may seem similar to our own, but it is the atmosphere of the place that is so very different. A north-facing coastline is novel for a south-coaster like me, and what a wonderfully wild and untamed coast it is. The saltings and mudflats seem to stretch almost to the horizon at low tide, for mile after mile after mile. There is so much space, so much wilderness, so many birds. Clouds of Dunlins, Knots, Sanderlings, Golden, Grey and Ringed Plovers, godwits, Curlews, Oystercatchers and Redshanks wheel above the distant tideline. Winter brings huge flocks of Brent Geese to join them on the mudflats or to swarm across the grazing meadows.

After a day spent out on the marshes, the little red brick and flint villages strung along their landward edge always look so cosy and inviting. The houses seem to be huddled together for warmth against the cold offshore wind. Salthouse, Cley, Blakeney, Morston, Stiffkey – evocative names to any birdwatcher, they draw me back again and again. But just as travel provides me with vital new experiences and challenges, so it also gives me a break from the old and familiar, enabling me to return to the same subjects year after year, to re-work them in the light of accumulated experience.

Storlek 11.7.93   Robert L. Greenhalf

Of things to come

Even in the middle of winter a sunny, blue-skied day can hold the promise of spring to come – at least for a short while. The 2nd February was one such day, in the remote heart of Romney Marsh.

> "A Peregrine skirts the Marsh, only a few feet above the ground, then rises to perch on a telegraph pole. Over the flood to the south, huge flocks of Lapwings wheel, perhaps ten thousand strong. They are jumpy, taking to the air at the slightest disturbance. Through the 'scope, I can make out about fifty Bewick's Swans, their fluting calls drift to me on the wind, mingled with the bright whistles of Wigeon and the nasal honks of Greylags. The swans are in spring mood, chasing and posturing, as are a dozen Coots on a broad, reed-fringed dyke just in front of me. They threaten and paddle frantically across the water with wings raised above backs, like sailing boats, uttering sharp metallic 'chink' calls, or patter across the water in hot pursuit of a rival with wings flailing, but I see no serious fighting.
>
> All becomes quiet as the light drops and a ringtail harrier quarters a nearby reedy dyke. A Barn Owl appears briefly behind the pool, working along an old inning wall that takes it out to where the Bewick's Swans are still calling."

On 17th February, in spite of an uncomfortably strong wind, passions were stirring on the open beachlands of Rye Harbour.

> "Above the flat beach, still streaked with flood water, Shelducks are chasing. They circle the pool several times with wild exuberance, accompanied by cackling and whistling calls, before landing on the water with much splashing, ducking and head-bobbing. The mood seems infectious, for on a neighbouring field of winter wheat, male Grey Partridges are defending their harems. With heads held high, legs a-blur, they shoot across the field at an astounding speed to confront rival males."

But it is not until the end of March, with the first of the summer migrants here, that spring can be heralded with any confidence.

> "A flock of thirty-five Sandwich Terns are on a low island at the east end of Ternery Pool – rather distant, but I draw and paint them through the 'scope. It is marvellous to see them back. There is much calling and flying around but little displaying as yet. They seem to be resting rather than settling in; perhaps they will move on."

One year later, to the day, on 29th March, my first Swallow of the year winged in from the south, low over our roof.

11·3·94 Ternery Pool Rye Harbour

Another bright but breezy day. Black-headed Gulls
are really getting in the mood for
breeding with much posturing &
displaying, chasing & squabbling
all accompanied by raucous cries.
About half of the Gulls are
in Summer Plumage, but those
that still have the white heads of
Winter seem equally enthusiastic in their displays.

2 ♂ Ruddy Duck
Still present.

Wings are made much use of in
Black-headed Gull display - held out
from the body at the front but tips
crossed still at the back.

Rabbits feed amongst the high-tide
Oystercatcher roost. Their soft shapes &
colours contrast with the sharp shapes
& black & white of the birds.
An interesting idea for
a watercolour? An adult
Mediterranean Gull
seen briefly.

1st chiffchaff
heard today!

13

14

14 · 3 · 94 Romney House

Superb displays of
Primroses & Celandines
along hedge bottom.
Surprising number
of bumble bees &
bee flies - with
hovering flight
& long
needle - like
proboscis
probing the
flowers

Scots Float 25.3.94
Scattered Rookery of perhaps a
hundred nests along half a mile of the
ancient cliff line that borders Romney Marsh.
Much squabbling & nest building.

16

Light bounces off
backs & wings of Rooks.
Jackdaws greyer —
reflect less light.

17·3·94 Saltburn
A mixed flock of Rooks, Jackdaws
& Crows enthusiastically digging in a
recently drilled field.

Two herons land in a field of winter
wheat, the bright green a perfect complement
to their purple grey.

17

30·3·94 Ternery Pool Rye Harbour

Two, occasionally three Ringed Plovers
chasing in the air & running on the
Shingle. They appear to be ♂♂ presumably
in territorial disputes. Much 'stiff-
winged' flight & along with more usual
calls, a low grating sound, rather Turnstone-
like which I don't recall hearing
before.

Sea-Kale is bursting forth
magnificent magenta & purple
shoots from dead-looking tubers.

25·4·94   Starlock, Playden   11·00 – 13·00   Bright & sunny, but with increasing S.W. Wind
Lambing field, many ewes with lambs, others about to give birth.   Rooks, Crows & Herring Gulls
attracted by the afterbirths. Rooks seem to be feeding mainly on insects attracted by sheep dung.

April

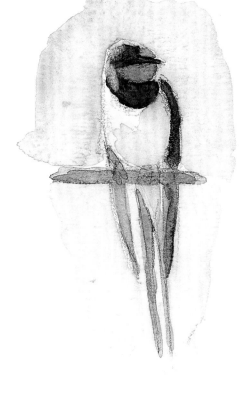

Extract from my diary for 5th April.

"The past few days of hazy, dewy dawns and warm sunny days have kick-started spring, propelling us towards the summer ahead. There will be setbacks of course, but the momentum seems unstoppable now. Explosions of spring green punctuate hedgerow and wood-edge where a week ago only the faintest hint of green washed the purples and browns of winter and splashes of white blackthorn blossom replace the fading cream of pussy willow in the hedgerows."

Insects suddenly abound. Mosquitoes dance in the warm evenings, hoverflies patrol, and large bumblebees hurtle and blunder amongst the primroses and bluebells. Tortoiseshell, Peacock and Small White butterflies enliven the garden. The Chiffchaffs, soloists in the blustery days of March, have to compete now with a swelling tide of birdsong. Blackbirds, Song Thrushes, Greenfinches, Linnets, Robins, Wrens, Dunnocks and Great Tits are all singing lustily now as I write at midday. Earlier, the thin, tuneless ditty of a Goldcrest came from the *Cupressus* and a Swallow added a cascade of liquid notes. The Starling that has laid its customary claim to our roof-space brought a medley of sounds gleaned from the winter marshes – the *chink* of Coot, piping of Redshank, *pee-wit* of Lapwing, quack of Mallard and whistle of Wigeon. There is a flurry of nest-building in the early mornings when the dew renders the materials more pliable.

Two weeks later, winter is having a final fling.

"Blossom cascades from the old pear tree. It escaped last night's frost which struck the grassy hollows white. The late afternoon sun shines through the fresh half-opened oak leaves, turning them to gold against the thunder-grey clouds. Today has been typical April – sunshine and showers – the sun, when it shone, the more intense for the rain. Willow Warblers and Blackcaps sang in the warm shelter of the overgrown hedge this morning and a pair of Swallows have been mating on the wires, but no signs yet of Whitethroats or Cuckoos. It has been a cold and mainly dull Easter with snow in the north and perhaps this has kept the birds further south. The hawthorn, in full leaf now, has flower buds, waiting for May."

6.4.94   Narrow Pits Rye Harbour   10·30 – 1330

Beautiful morning, slight breeze bringing the occasional
sad, sweet descending cadences of the first Willow Warbler
of the year across the water. Two pairs of Great Crested Grebes
displaying, including once the 'weed dance' where both partners
dive & reappear with strands of aquatic vegetation in their
beak. They approach and move bills from side to side in a
stylized way, the weed soon being dropped. Much diving,
preening & chasing of rival pairs.

Robert R. Greenhalf

24

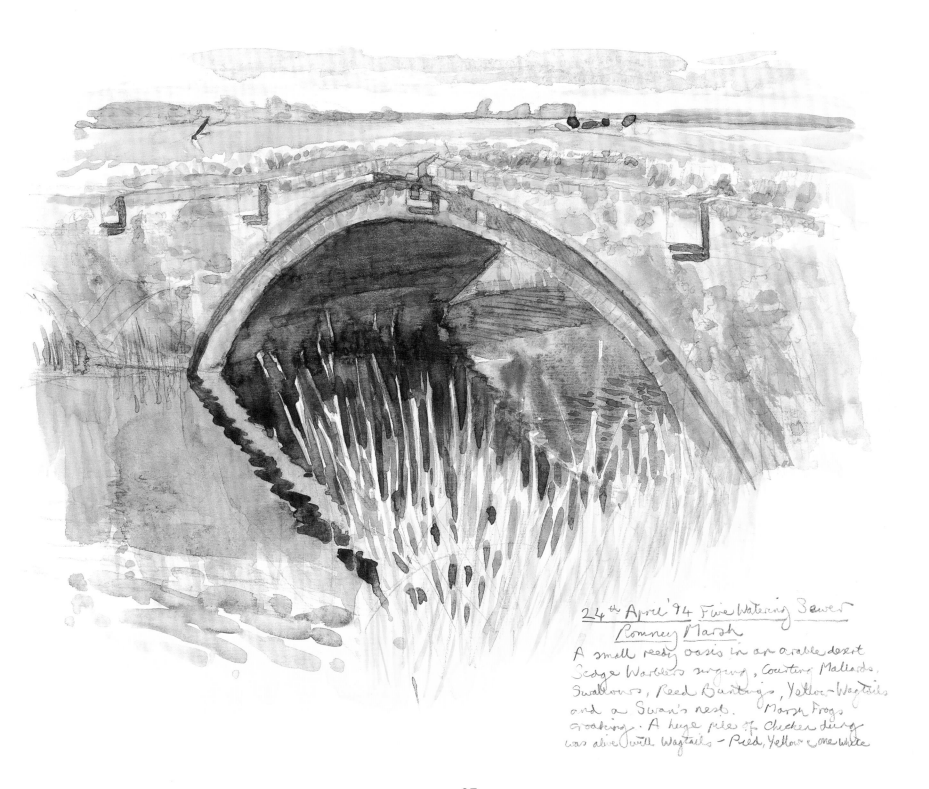

24th April '94 Five Watering Sewer
Romney Marsh
A small reedy oasis in an arable desert
Sedge Warblers singing, Courting Mallards,
Swallows, Reed Buntings, Yellow Wagtails
and a Swan's nest. Marsh Frogs
croaking. A huge pile of chicken dung
was alive with Wagtails - Pied, Yellow one white

Spring migration – Bardsey

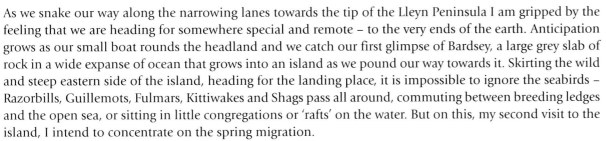

As we snake our way along the narrowing lanes towards the tip of the Lleyn Peninsula I am gripped by the feeling that we are heading for somewhere special and remote – to the very ends of the earth. Anticipation grows as our small boat rounds the headland and we catch our first glimpse of Bardsey, a large grey slab of rock in a wide expanse of ocean that grows into an island as we pound our way towards it. Skirting the wild and steep eastern side of the island, heading for the landing place, it is impossible to ignore the seabirds – Razorbills, Guillemots, Fulmars, Kittiwakes and Shags pass all around, commuting between breeding ledges and the open sea, or sitting in little congregations or 'rafts' on the water. But on this, my second visit to the island, I intend to concentrate on the spring migration.

Memories of my first visit come flooding back as old familiar sights and sounds greet us – the incessant bickering of Oystercatchers, the moaning of seals, and sheep everywhere. A Little Owl scolds from a stone wall as we approach Ty Bach where I am staying with old friends Kim Atkinson and Gwydd Morley. Kim, who has spent much of her life on Bardsey, is an artist of great talent and originality. Her bold watercolours and woodcuts are a powerful evocation of life on the island that she knows so intimately.

A misty drizzle hangs over the island next morning as we set out on a reconnaissance. The sweet heavy scent of gorse fills the air as we zigzag our way up the mountain. As we reach the 500ft 'summit' a Peregrine hangs almost motionless in the keen updraught. Below, the steep northern slopes are dotted with nesting Lesser Black-backed Gulls, handsome with charcoal-grey backs and yellow legs. To the south and west the rough gorse and heather anarchy of the hillside yields to the smooth-grazed patchwork of fields. Everywhere there is rock: outcrops, cliffs and boulders, stone walls and buildings, binding and domesticating the landscape.

"The Peregrine half closes its wings, surges forward, checks momentarily, then with wings stream-lined flat against body, it accelerates into a dramatic swoop that takes it away to the south. We take the same direction, descending more slowly to the fields below where Choughs and Oyster-catchers probe the close-cropped turf and Wheatears and Jackdaws hunt insects amongst the sheep droppings. A huge Raven with controlled, powerful wingbeats flies towards the lighthouse."

Set on the low rocky southern tip of Bardsey, the red-and-white striped lighthouse is a potential death-trap for incoming migrants on dark, cloudy or misty nights. Attracted like moths to a candle, they circle the light until they drop exhausted or dash themselves against the tower. Floodlighting the tower and neighbouring areas of gorse on nights when an 'attraction' is predicted helps to cut the mortality.

"On the sheltered west side of the island Wheatears flit from every field and Whimbrels trill as they move between land and shore. Pied and White Wagtails and Rock Pipits complete the scene. Lapwings display over sedgy fields, Oystercatchers pipe a warning. We follow the coast round to the northwest corner where the rather cramped seawatching hide at least provides some relief from the rain and wind, and close views of Whimbrels on the rocks, and Gannets passing close inshore."

Birds are coming and going all the time on Bardsey, their movements governed mainly by the weather. Day two, the 30th April, dawned with low cloud obscuring the mountain and a keen southerly wind. There seemed to be Willow Warblers everywhere, in the gorse, along the walls and more surprisingly on the beach. Still more unexpected was a dapper male Pied Flycatcher that stood out, sharp black and white against the pink rock. On the fields around the lighthouse were masses of Wheatears and small flocks of Whimbrels and Dunlins. A female Sparrowhawk exploded from a gorse bush, leaving behind a pile of buff and grey feathers, from a Wheatear, perhaps. At another bush sat a smart male Whinchat.

A change in the weather means a change of birds. Warm and sunny conditions set in for the remainder of the week bringing Sedge Warblers, Blackcaps, Lesser Whitethroats and the rarity of the week, a vagrant Subalpine Warbler from southern Europe. A White Stork and a couple of Goshawks pass through in the next couple of days, but they do not linger long and I miss them. Willow Warblers become scarce, but on the flat field near the landing place and on the sandy beach of Porth Solfach, newly arrived wagtails and pipits chase insects amongst the sheep. There are three Blue-headed Wagtails, one of which is a superb male with bright sulphur-yellow underparts, striking pale blue head, and olive-green back. White Wagtails are here in good numbers along with a few Pieds and two boldly-streaked Tree Pipits.

Swifts, swallows and martins stream through now, taking advantage of the kind weather. A Cuckoo, perched on a fence at the north end of the island seems to be practising its call rather unsuccessfully.

A Nightingale is trapped at the Bird Observatory on the morning of our departure. It is a rarity here and we go to see it in the hand and, after watching its release and its distinctive orange tail disappearing into a bush, we make our own sad farewells.

3rd May '95   Bardsey - North end . Several Whimbrel on the rocks, all depart
on my approach except one . Impressive waves breaking behind the bird as
the tide flows .

4th May '95 Bardsey. A collapsed stone Gateway, soft early morning light behind.
The field strewn with sheep droppings, is alive with wheatears. Swallows & martins
stream overhead, with a few Swifts. Choughs swoop from the hillside where they feed,
to their nest in the sea cliffs.

4th May '95 Solfach, Bardsey
Very Hot afternoon. A Ewe & lambs rest on the beach.
The beach alive with wagtails - Mainly White with a few
Pied & Yellows - they are 'jumping' for flies. Too hot to
Complete the painting in one sitting, I seek the shade for an hour
before continuing.

5th May '95   Bardsey. looking North   from the Henllwyn, early morning.

11.5.95 Rye Harbour Ternery Pool   Robert B R Greenhalf

The desert blooms

The shingle ridges that were swept bare by the winter's gales are alive again – crowned by huge waxy-leaved clumps of Sea Kale and carpeted with purple and mauve flowered Ivy-leaved Toadflax and Sea Pea, and lemon-yellow Wall Pepper. Blue and purple spikes of Viper's Bugloss, pink Valerian, Yellow Horned Poppies and dozens of ther plants make the desert bloom for a few short weeks – an amazing sight. The light has an intensity that can dazzle, for it bounces back from the pebbles.

Little Terns animate the sky with their jerky, angular flight and stabbing calls. Any large gull foolish enough to cross the ridges where they nest runs the gauntlet of dive-bombing terns, but they seem less effective against foxes, Little Owls and, particularly, Kestrels that in recent years have taken a heavy toll of the chicks. Oystercatchers and Ringed Plovers share the open shingle with the Little Terns. A few pairs of Wheatears nest in rabbit burrows or in artificially constructed sites, but most activity centres on the Ternery and Wader Pools.

On 11th May I spent a couple of hours at my favourite time of day, watching and painting from the Parkes hide at the eastern end of Ternery Pool.

> "Soft evening backlight; the small island in front of me alive with squabbling Black-headed Gulls' nests, some with eggs visible. Behind them, Sandwich Terns rest, preen and court on the shingle margin. Over on the larger island cluster many more Sandwich Terns and gulls, including a single Mediterranean Gull. Four or five Black-headed Gulls have built nests in a row on a floating plank that is anchored in the reed margin. Pandemonium breaks out when a Herring Gull raids the colony. It seems to be very determined, eating eggs in spite of being constantly buffeted by the smaller gulls."

By the beginning of June there is a continual procession of terns from the sea to the pool, bringing fish for their young, whose begging cries add to the already considerable melee. But there are other species quietly raising their young in the reedy margins of Ternery Pool. Great Crested Grebes dive for fish for their stripy-necked youngsters. Tiny Little Grebe chicks are being fed insects picked from the surface or plucked from the air. Flotillas of piebald Shelducklings move in ordered lines across the pool, watchful parents at front and rear. Ruddy Ducks are less regimented; both adults and young seem to spend as much time under water as they do on top. The nearby wader pool is shallow and muddy with a luxuriance of vegetation and has no nesting gulls or terns. On the beautiful sunny evening of 6th July I was watching from the hide.

> *"A couple of pairs of Ringed Plovers chase around; one has a single chick, now fairly independent, running here and there at great speed on legs too big for the tiny piebald ball of fluff that is its body. One parent keeps a watchful eye on it and later broods it, her breast feathers fluffed out like a tent, the youngster just visible beneath. A pair of Oystercatchers have one rather gawky, unadventurous offspring that sticks close to its parents and moves very cautiously compared to the plover chick. There are also several well-grown Redshank chicks.*
>
> *A Kestrel hovering nearby triggers alarm signals from the Redshanks and anxious notes from the Ringed Plovers, whose chick responds by crouching. As the evening wears on the number of Rabbits around the edge of the pool increases. Their ears are orange where the light shines through from behind. Their soft, rounded, dun-coloured forms make an interesting contrast to the animated angularity of the birds."*

The resident birds here may still be preoccupied with rearing young, but six Dunlins, quietly feeding in the margins, are a sign that autumn passage has already begun.

1 May 15.

Several pairs of
Little Tern apparently
setting. Still much
courtship activity with
many birds carrying
sand eels to their mates.

A pair of Oystercatchers would
come & settle on a particular
spot on the beach, but they would
be absent for long periods so
can't think that they are
incubating.

Quite a lot of aggressive
chasing amongst the Ringed
Plover. Several well
grown chicks present.

Rye Harbour 3·6·93   15·00 - 18·00   Ternwatch caravan.

chicks ⇗

Robert R. Greenhalf

Ternery Pool, Rye Harbour
3·6·93   19:00 - 21:45
Watching from Parkes hide.
There is a pair of Great
Crested Grebes with two
well grown young. The
adults seem intent on
sleep but the young have
other ideas! They prod
their parents who either
respond aggressively or reluctantly
dive for fish.

The Little Grebes have two offspring.
There is a 'hatch' of insects in front of the
hide, sheltered from the strong E. Wind & the
adults dart back & forth picking them from
the surface or sometimes
out of the air.

Although both the same size
only one chick is being fed,
the other hunts its own prey.

Robert R. Greenhalf

7ᵗʰ June '94   Temery Pool Rye Harbour   17·00 - 19·00 hrs
Several pairs of Common Terns with small chicks on low islands at the west
end of the pool. Strong S.W. Wind; light from left and behind. Terns brooding young
face away from the wind, with chicks under wings. Plumage of adults much
ruffled.

18·00   Light now almost directly behind birds, much white reflecting off water and
shingle.   Black headed Gulls seem to cluster together more than the terns, taking
advantage of shelter from the wind provided by their fellows.

16th June '94 Rye Harbour looking N.W. 21·00 hrs. colours heightened by the setting sun.

Robert R. Greenhalf.

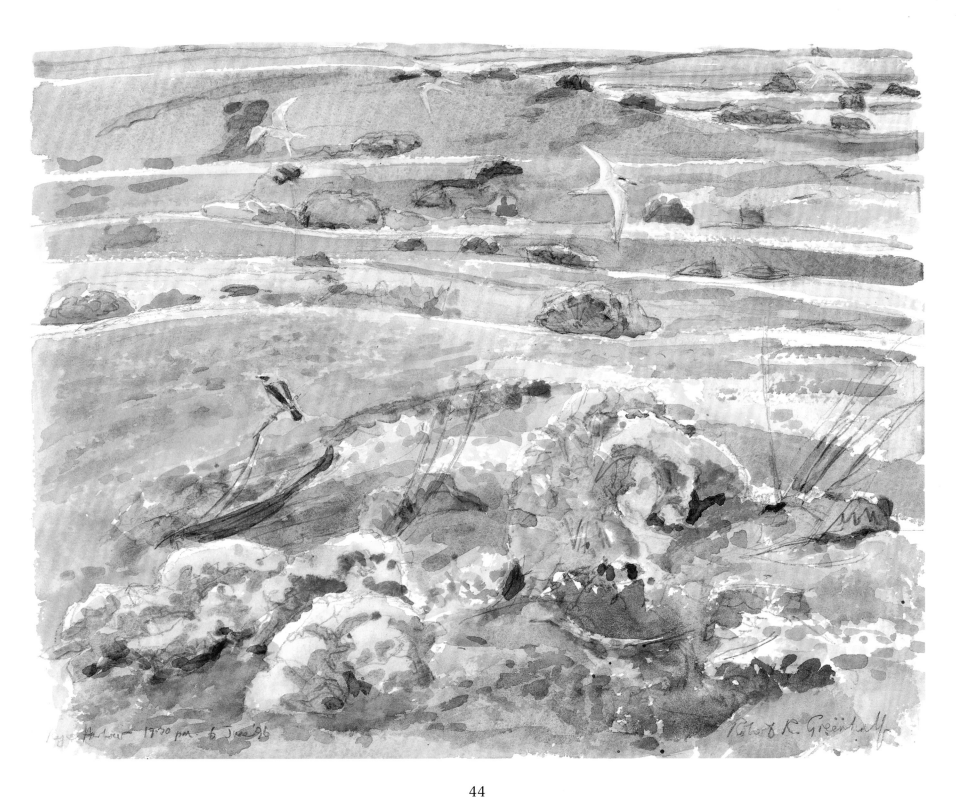

Hayle Harbour 19:30 pm 6 June 96   Robert K. Greenhalf

Midsummer marsh

As June progresses the marsh becomes daily more heavy with luxuriant growth. The reed-fringed dykes which drain, irrigate and divide the levels resound to the harsh chattering of Reed and Sedge Warblers, while cock Reed Buntings proclaim from the bleached survivors of last year's growth. Over most of the marsh, heavily grazed by sheep or under intensive arable crops, bird life is fairly limited. You can add to the list Moorhen, Corn Bunting, Yellow Wagtail, Mute Swan and Mallard, and post-breeding flocks of Lapwings and Starlings, but there is not the variety of species that winter brings. Fortunately, a few conservation-minded landowners have raised water levels to recreate the sort of wet meadow and shallow water areas that must have existed on the lowest areas of the marsh before the advent of modern pump drainage.

Birds take readily to such areas. Redshank, Lapwing and Snipe, Mallard, Teal, Shoveler, and perhaps even Garganey are possible breeding species, and there are sometimes surprises. For example on 7th June:

> *"A Hobby beats low across the meadows above sheep and bullocks. Reminiscent of a winter's Peregrine or Merlin it, too, lifts the Starlings and Lapwings. At the winter flood, now a sea of long grass with patches of water and mud, there are Shelducks, several pairs of Shovelers, Mallard and Greylag Geese, Grey Herons and, on the far side, a sleeping Spoonbill."*

On 5th July a Hobby is still present, now hunting the numerous dragonflies, and the autumn wader passage has already begun.

> *"Three magnificent summer-plumaged Spotted Redshanks and two Greenshanks feed in the shallows or rest amongst the herons and egrets. Ruffs, still in partial summer plumage, sit and feed with a flock of Lapwings. Beyond, a 'sedge' of herons are sleeping or preening, purple-grey against the richness of greens, ochres and siennas of the summer marsh. A female Marsh Harrier lazily quarters in the shimmering haze, occasionally flopping untidily into the reeds. A fox disappears into the tall vegetation, its progress marked only by alarmed birds.*
>
> *As evening approaches and I walk back to the car two hares appear on the edge of a pea field ahead of me. They seem unconcerned by my presence, in no hurry to get out of my way, preoccupied with each other. A Barn Owl drifts silently from the derelict cottage and out over a field of wheat as the light fades."*

47

Corn Bunting

Inner premaries
Moulted

20th June '94

Romney Marsh - reed bed
with some open water on the
South side and rough pasture
with sheep. Moderate S.W.
wind e impressive purple
- grey clouds.

A fence is popular with
singing Corn Buntings and
Yellow wagtails - the Bunting
'squats on its haunches' on
the fence posts, the wagtail
prefers the barbed wire.

Lapwings are
already flocking -
there are 80
together with the sheep
Several moorhens e
coots have families in
the reed edge e a
redshank is holding
territory in the pasture.
Kingfisher also seen.
A rather tatty of
Marsh/Harrier quarters
the pasture.

20th June 94 Romney House
Long grass areas are a rich tapestry
Pale purples & browns of grass seed—
heads complement the greens. Highlights
provided by yellows & whites of buttercups
& oxeyes, reds of dock.

28th June '94 New Gate Winchelsea

Hot, cloudless day, slight S. breeze
Sheep visibly parting (still with full
fleeces here) some lying in the shade
of an ancient hedge bank.

Marsh Frogs sun bathing, hauled
out on a mat of dead sedges
in the middle of a drainage ditch.
Some very large, perhaps 4" from
tip of nose to tail. Ditch nearly
choked with sedges & pond weeds

2nd August '94 Pett Level

Sultry Summer's afternoon
A mute Swan family paddle
lazily in a shallow pool.
Sand Martins, the first of huge flocks
that roost in the reeds here in the Autumn,
hawk for insects low over the water.
Emperor Dragonflies, apple green
& cerulean, patrol the dykes where
a few spikes of the exquisite Flowering
Rush bloom & Moorhens bicker &
scuttle for cover as I approach.

10th June '94
Military Canal,
Winchelsea.
Constant chattering
of Sedge & Reed
Warblers from small
reed bed. Yellow Flag
Irises magnificent.

Sedge Warbler

Seabirds and seals

By midsummer migration on Bardsey has slowed to a trickle and it is the cliffs with their breeding seabirds that are my main preoccupation. It takes a good head for heights and a fair amount of nerve to reach the best vantage points from which to draw them. A narrow path, little more than a sheep track, traverses the steep eastern slopes of the 'mountain' linking the scattered colonies of Razorbills, Guillemots, Kittiwakes, Shags and Fulmars on the cliffs below. Birds can be seen coming and going from the path, but to see them on their ledges a further scramble is called for. Often this unavoidably takes you through one of the numerous Herring or Lesser Black-backed Gull colonies that favour the cliff-top slopes. At this time of year, with young to defend, you run the gauntlet of dive-bombing attacks and verbal abuse from the adults.

As you near the cliff edge a cacophony of nasal brayings, gruntings and wild, disconcertingly child-like cries build up to a crescendo as suddenly you find yourself looking down on a scene that at once mesmerises, excites and inspires. It is daunting in its complexity. How can I convey all this richness of sights, sounds and smells with just a few sheets of paper?

The cliffs here are predominantly blue-grey or black with occasional patches of salmon-pink and white veins of quartz. In places the grey is enlivened by bright orange or pale grey-green lichens. Below the high-water mark encrustations of barnacles suck the colour from the rock, turning it to pale ochre. Thongs of wrack are anchored to submerged rocks. Where they swirl in the underwater currents the deep aqua and indigo is shot with purple and a deep, rich brown.

The hard, angular rocks and their shadows provide the backdrop against which hundreds of birds move to and fro, an endlessly changing pattern of shapes and colours. Kittiwakes spiral in the upcurrents, pale grey shapes against the dark sea. Torpedo-bodied Razorbills and Guillemots fly back and forth. Better adapted to life in the sea, their rather small paddle-like wings have to work overtime to support their heavy bodies in the air. Although superficially similar in appearance, their nesting habits are totally different. The Guillemots pack together in rows on the narrow open ledges, whereas the more compact and dapper Razorbills choose the seclusion of crevices under the larger boulders. Glossy, dark green Shags build untidy nests on some of the widest ledges, often with Guillemots as neighbours, whereas Fulmars are more solitary, preferring individual nooks near the cliff-tops.

Beneath the seabird cliffs there will often be a seal or two 'bottling', but the best place to see them on Bardsey is in the sheltered bay known as the Henllwyn. Here they haul out on the rocks, a dozen or two together of assorted sizes and colours. They always look and sound most uncomfortable, constantly shifting position whilst uttering heartfelt moans and sighs. In the water they seem much more at home, able to relax and luxuriate in their element.

9th July 1994 Bardsey Island   12 noon - 18.00 hrs

As the tide drops the Grey Seals rest up on the wrack covered rocks. They constantly change position, raise their heads, yawn or scrap with their neighbours, all accompanied by moans, sighs or snorts. Flippers are used little in this manoeuvring except when in a hurry to reach the water when disturbed. More leisurely changes of position are achieved by arching the back or shifting body weight, quivering ripples are clearly visible travelling along the length of the animal. They seem to like to keep within a few feet of the sea, so move down the rocks as the tide ebbs.

6th July '94 p.m. Bardsey Island - The Henllwyn

A group of Oystercatchers are resting & preening on the wrack-shrouded rocks –
an irresistible subject. Oystercatchers are Bardsey, you can never be out of earshot
of their incessant bickering.

　　　As the flowing tide lifts the wrack from the rocks, they depart for the fields
leaving me to draw an inquisitive seal that is eyeing me lazily as she apparently
luxuriates in the water, occasionally snorting, with pleasure?

6th July '94 Bardsey Island

A morning of sunshine and showers. Looking S.W. to rocks off-shore where seals are hauled up, their mournful wails drift across to me, mingled with the cries of Curlews & the ever-present bickering of Oystercatchers. As rain approaches from the East the sea takes on a dark viridian hue.

5th July '94 Bardsey - Kittiwake Colony   Robert R. Greenhalf

60

8th July · Bardsey Island

Late afternoon. A Shag's nest
surrounded by ledges packed with
Guillemots, some with their own
half-grown chicks. They are in
a sheltered gully with a rock overhang
'roof'. The ledges, whitewashed with
droppings reflect the blue of the sky; the
vertical planes pick up a warm ochre glow
from the sun baked stone where I sit.

Tea on the veranda

I usually regret it if I venture onto our veranda without binoculars and a sketch book. True, a quick ten minute break can very soon extend to an hour or more as I become absorbed in watching a Green Woodpecker in the oak tree, or a Hobby catching dragonflies above the garden, but what, after all, is the point in having a veranda if you cannot find time to enjoy it? We have sat on the veranda in every month of the year, for it is generally sheltered from the wind and, on a sunny day, it can be warm even in winter. In summer I practically live out there, when I am not out 'in the field'. It is often the sounds of birds that you pick up on at this season of the year.

On 7th July heavy black clouds threatened rain at mid-morning and I noted the following:

"A Turtle Dove crooned earlier, now a Chiffchaff sings, but somehow not with the same enthusiasm of the spring birds. There are Magpies chattering from the oak trees, youngsters, full grown save for a few inches of tail, following their parents in a garrulous posse and I fear for the Song Thrush who perches briefly with worms for her young. Starlings, noisy as ever, descend on the field below. A Pheasant's crow is answered by our neighbour's Bantam cock. Incessant chirping from sparrows and 'cheeps' come from the Greenfinches in the hedge. A brood of recently fledged Swallows twitters from the wires, and Woodpigeons coo lazily."

Three weeks later, on 28th July, it is sights rather than sounds that catch my attention.

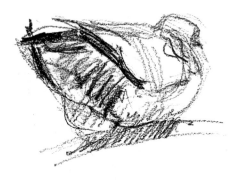

"9.00 a.m. and it is already hot and sultry, following the pattern of the past few weeks. There must be a hatch of storm flies, for fifty or so Black-headed Gulls are engaged in aerobatics at roof height. Two Spotted Flycatchers are after the same prey, using the dead twigs of the almond tree as a vantage point. Later, at 7.00 p.m., I'm on the veranda again when five very white birds plane down and land on the parched sheep pasture just beyond the river. I rush to the studio for binoculars, returning just in time to confirm that they are Little Egrets as they take to the wing again and head downstream. As the evening sun turns the wheat fields to bronze, a Hobby circles low over the old cliff line, occasionally grabbing at dragonflies with its feet."

Pupil brown in Juvenile,
white in Adult.

17th June '94 Romney House

An adult and a juvenile
Green Woodpecker, first seen
anting in the field, later
flew to the oak tree.
Although fully grown, the
young bird was still being
fed ants by its parent,
although in the tree it
appeared to be finding its own
food as I watched it extracting
a moth from a crevice.
Adult more wary than youngster,
tending to keep to the shadows.

20·5·94 Romney House A Starling's nest in
dead branch of oak tree raided by
a Little Owl. Starlings frantic,
young presumably eaten by owl.

3rd August '94 Romney House

Evening. The setting sun casts long shadows of trees across the nearly-ripe corn field. Warm e still. A Turtle Dove croons from the hedge e a frenzy of Swallows draws my attention to a ♂ Sparrowhawk slipping low along the hedgeline.

Passing strangers

It is usually towards the middle of July when I first become aware that the autumn wader passage has begun. It is then that I hear the first thin lisping calls of Common Sandpipers or the urgent *tu-tu* of Greenshanks' drifting cries from the river. August is well underway before I can detect the more discreet movements of warblers through the garden, for with Whitethroats, Lesser Whitethroats, Blackcaps and Willow Warblers all nesting here it is not easy to tell which are 'our' birds and which are migrants. However, some mornings the bushes seem alive with warblers and often there will be a stranger in their midst: a Garden Warbler, Spotted Flycatcher or Reed Warbler perhaps.

But it is the waders which capture my imagination each autumn – wanderers from their high Arctic breeding grounds, heading south to winter around the shores of Europe or Africa, stopping off here to rest and refuel. One of the best local staging posts is Pett Pools. I visited there on 17th July just one week after the Sussex Ornithological Society had lowered the water level of one of the roadside pools to create a muddy feeding area for migrant waders.

> *"Nine Black-tailed Godwits, all except one still in stunning breeding plumage with brick-red fronts and boldly streaked and barred backs, are resting and preening in the shallow water. The odd-bird-out, in the subtle greys of winter plumage, looks like a different species. There is a Ruff, too, which still sports prominent cream feathering around the neck, vestiges of his breeding plumage.*
>
> *A Greenshank appears mid-afternoon, feeds briefly, then sleeps for the remaining two hours of my stay, no doubt tired after a long journey. Nine Common Sandpipers actively skitter and bob their way around the weedy margins of the pool, which are also favoured by three Little Ringed Plovers. A trio of trilling Whimbrels circle the pool but do not land, continuing westwards instead."*

For the next couple of months the pool will be busy with the comings and goings of various waders, with peak numbers in late August and early September. Typically about twenty-five species, plus one or two rarities, will be involved, but numbers of individual species vary considerably from year to year. By the end of September passage is more or less over and the water level has often recovered, drowning the mud. On 20th September I visited in the early evening for an hour:

> *"There is still enough margin to attract Dunlins, a few Snipe and a Ruff. Swallows and Sand Martins hawk low over the water, dodging between the Mallard, Teal and Shovelers that are scattered across the surface.*
>
> *More Swallows are on the seaward side of the wall, streaming north-east along the coast, low over the heads of huge Great Black-backed Gulls that sit on the last exposed rocks, watching the flowing tide till they, too, are pushed off and head for their roost on Camber Sands.*
>
> *The tide brings more waders to the pool margins – a single Black-tailed Godwit sleeps on one leg, an animated group of Redshanks bathe and preen, and Curlews fly overhead to the fields behind."*

Tern Pool
Rye Harbour 23·7·93

Bob J R Greenhalf

7th September '94 Romney House

Still, hazy, sultry damp autumn morning.
Gossamer threads drifting by.
   A garrulous, restless party of Starlings
whirl into the elder bush, gorge themselves
on the grape-black berries for a
minute before whisking off on a
whim to return half an hour
later.
   Aeshna dragonflies thread the
spaces between hedge & house;
blood red Sympetrum sun themselves
on rocks between hunting forays.
   Plump Blackcaps & lesser
Whitethroats in the elderbush
betray themselves with the
occasional harsh
"tac tac".

7th September '94. River Piter about a quarter of a mile upstream of Starlock. Evening, the sun soon to sink behind the old cliff line. Bright with a fresh S.W. wind rippling the surface of the river.

Aeshna Dragonflies rest in sunny spots out of the wind, Swallows battle against it. There are still a couple of Whinchats in the field near the locks, they have been there since the 26th of August.

Peter & R. Greenhalf

77

Mecca

As a fledgling birdwatcher in the 1960s the North Norfolk coast, centred on the small village of Cley, was Mecca, for here, it seemed, more rare birds were seen than at any other spot in the entire country. Autumn was *the* time to be there. Those long weekends crammed with dawn-to-dusk birding, evenings in 'The George' and sleeping rough on Salthouse Heath are but distant memories now, but in recent years I have managed to visit again once or twice each year. It is not so much the prospect of rare birds that draws me there now – more the wild spirit of the place, those wonderful wide endless sweeps of saltmarsh and mud, the cosy red brick and flint villages to the landward, and creeks winding to the distant sea where seals haul out on sandbanks – all of this and more besides, plus, of course, the birds as icing on the cake.

Thankfully I no longer have to sleep rough, for my sister, Mary Bonham, and family live conveniently nearby. It was with my brother-in-law, Pat, that I spent the 11th September birdwatching at Cley.

" *Warm, sun and cloud, with a light north-west wind from the sea and a heat haze over the land when the sun is out.*

We start at Teal Hide. There are masses of birds on Pat's Pool in front of us: feral Greylags, Whitefronts, Canada and Egyptian Geese, many Ruffs, four Greenshanks, a Spotted Redshank, small restless flocks of Little Stints – perhaps forty or fifty in total – and numerous Dunlins and Lapwings. Ducks are here in good numbers too – many Teal and Wigeon with smaller numbers of Pintail and Gadwall. At Cley Eye we eat sandwiches on the beach as a well-marked immature Little Gull flies west close in, followed later by a young Gannet. Otherwise, apart from a few Kittiwakes and terns, the sea seems rather quiet.

The North Hide is crowded for there are three Red-necked Phalaropes swimming in the shallow water. Looking rather like dainty miniature versions of Black-headed Gulls, they move rapidly over the surface, frequently changing direction at an instant to pick an insect from the surface with a needle-fine bill. We have close but rather brief views, against the light, but there is, in any case, no room to draw. There is not much to be seen on Arnold's Marsh, except for an adult Little Gull amongst some Black-headed Gulls.

Returning to Cley Eye along the sea wall, a splendid Arctic Skua attacks a Sandwich Tern close in, and a couple more Gannets head West. The skua's flight is powerful and controlled; it follows the contours of the waves, only inches above the surface, then rises to attack from below."

I did little drawing, just a quick sketch of the skua and tern, for it was a day for walking and watching – a 'day off', but the opportunity to draw the phalaropes presented itself again later in the week when the hide was less crowded.

On that day, the 15th, a Redstart flitted from post to post in front of me as I walked to the hide beneath the sea wall and later, on my return, a Pied Flycatcher was using the old blockhouse near the 'Eye' as a vantage point. Five Lapland Buntings were feeding unobtrusively around the edge of the nearby pool and I just had to make some sketches of them in spite of a light drizzle that had set in.

The day before I was sitting at the seaward end of the East Bank, Cley, drawing the landscape across Arnold's Marsh, when a Short-eared Owl apparently flew in from the sea, low over my head, to land a couple of hundred yards beyond me in a field. It sat in the open, staring around for some minutes as if to get its bearings, before moving to a more sheltered position nearby. A metallic *ping, ping* alerted me to the presence of a little flock of Bearded Tits that showed themselves briefly in the reed tops in spite of a moderate breeze. Seen against the low evening light, their tails were flashes of bright orange. A Kingfisher and a jet fighter plane simultaneously streaked across Arnold's Marsh on identical trajectories.

Last year it was the beginning of October before I managed to get to Cley for my autumn visit, and by then the departure of summer visitors and passage of waders was just about over; only a few stragglers remained. A Goldcrest, presumably newly arrived, searched amongst the wind-blown tangle of Horned Poppies in the lee of the sea wall, and the marshes seemed set for winter, loaded with ducks. The mudflats of Blakeney Harbour teemed with winter wader flocks: Curlews, Oystercatchers, Redshanks, Godwits, Grey Plovers, Knots, Ringed Plovers and Dunlins, and out above the distant tideline came the first wavering black line of returning Brent Geese.

81

White Wagtail - pale grey mantle, back & rump & pure white underparts & flanks.

6th October 1994 Blakeney Quay
Dull, moderate S.W. wind. 2 Pied
& 2 White Wagtails chasing insects amongst
the tide line debris in the beach Car Park.
The White Wagtails, more timid than the Pieds, soon left.
one had quite a bright yellow 'face'.

5th October 1974   16·30 – 1800
The wind dropped an hour before
sunset. Perfect calm. Three Hares
graze amongst Tussocks in a rough
field. A ♀ Sparrowhawk low over
the grass causes brief havoc amongst a
covey of Red-legged Partridges.
   Partly obscured by reeds, a Heron
preens, Cattle graze behind.

Teal & Lapwing have perfect reflections in the shallow pool
as the light fades.

A November day

Of course November can have bright and sunny days; indeed, this year there have been quite a few. Throughout an exceptionally mild, dry October, the trees remained stubbornly green, and the glorious golden days of autumn were postponed by a month. But this was unusual. Last year my diary records an afternoon's stroll around Pett Level on a more typical November day.

Extract from my diary for 26th November, 14.30–17.00.

"A dull, gloomy afternoon with light misty rain at times, like so many days this month. I set off from Winchelsea through the Medieval Arch, New Gate and on to Pett Level. As I strike south across the Levels towards the sea the light increases slightly and casts an eerie yellow glow that intensifies the green of the fields and the white of the sheep, lending a surreal quality to the landscape. Some of the main drainage dykes have been mechanically shorn of their vegetation, leaving bits of white shining roots and tubers to float on the brown surface. The rich red-brown of the reeds is a perfect foil to the bright green of the grass, the whole set off by the greys of sky and water."

A large flock of Rooks skirts the marsh and lands in the tall ash trees where they nest each spring. They are cawing enthusiastically; I can hear them quite clearly from half a mile away. Ahead, Lapwings fill the air. Several hundred strong and restless, they rise calling, move a few hundred yards and settle, only to rise again moments later. There are Curlews too, and smaller, swifter waders that punctuate the gloom with their more rapid flight and calls – Redshanks, Turnstones, Dunlins, Snipe, and a few Golden Plovers. Against the bright green fields the Lapwings look blue-grey, taking their colour from the sky. Five Brent Geese graze quietly, unmoved by the antics of the restless plovers all around them.

I mount the sea wall. The tide is in and no mud or rocks remain. On a calm sea there are a few Great Crested Grebes and masses of gulls, chevrons of which have been passing overhead since I left Winchelsea. Heading southwest along the shore I come to the pools. There is a smart drake Gadwall and a few Coots here, but little else to detain me. At Toot Rock I strike inland and follow the Royal Military Canal back to New Gate. Two Green Sandpipers rise in front of me, but alight again a few hundred yards further on. A pair of Stonechats top the highest bushes along the canal bank and the sharp *chit, chit* of a Grey Wagtail cuts the gloom.

In the middle of my path stands the huge yellow caterpillar-tracked machine used to clear the ditches and dykes. On its crane arm is a rake-like head with double scissor-teeth that sever the plant stems and roots. In its wake the canal banks lie shorn smooth, laid bare to the winter, divested of their summer clothing of rush and iris, sedge and loosestrife. Amongst the sprawl of dredged vegetation and mud lie the shells of freshwater mussels. They are big: four or five inches across, and they, too, lie open, silver-grey and mother-of-pearl, empty to the sky. Others bear the ragged holes pecked by herons or gulls, eager for a meal of the hapless molluscs.

The light starts to go rapidly as I cross a bridge, nearly back at Winchelsea. Pausing to look west along the canal, the scene is reduced to flat shapes in tones of grey, and a single light from a house on a distant hill is reflected in the water, like a Whistler nocturne.

14th October '94
Saltbarn Farm 15·30 – 17·30
Sitting on a straw bale in the middle of a stubble field.
Jays calling from all directions. Harsh scolding of
a Grey Squirrel from the ash tree in the hedge to my
left on inspection was caused by the presence of a Little Owl, heard
earlier. Redwings & siskins pass overhead. Rooks cawing in distance.

13th October 1994
Royal Military Canal at
Appledore 13.30 ~ 17.00

Hazy, warm sunny
afternoon. Six ♂♂
& 4 ♀♀ Mallard loaf
on the left bank in the
shade of overhanging
trees. From time to time
they take to the water
drawing & splashing

with much quacking.
Perched in the
overhang above, a Kingfisher
makes a few plunged dives
before heading off up stream.

Moorhen are numerous here -
perhaps a dozen visible on this stretch,
mainly juveniles. Still many dragonflies
hawking over the reeds.

Robert R. Greenhalf

87

9th November '94 Starlock

Mild, cloudy day with hints
of sun between clouds, rain
threatening from the East.
A ♀ Kestrel twice flew
across the river with a small
rodent. A Reed Bunting feeds
briefly on reed seeds nearby.
Still an Aeshna Dragonfly
patrolling the reed edge.

27th October '94

Ronney House
The late afternoon sun
casts long shadows & turns the
stubbles to gold.
  Jays are everywhere, screeching
as they fly from oak to oak, sometimes
up to four together.

7th October '93 Little Banks.
Greenfinches & an occasional Great Tit
feeding on ripe sunflower heads

16th November '94   Playden

Blackbirds & Thrushes rustle amongst
the dead chestnut leaves, the cock birds
scrapping when they get too close to one another.
Behind me two squirrels are heads down
amongst the leaves in the hedge bottom, searching
for nuts.
  A tiny Goldcrest appears in the Sycamore in front of
me & feverishly inspects the last few leaves before hurrying on
to the holly bush.

Winter sun

I find it hard to resist a bright sunny day even in the middle of winter. If I stay indoors I become edgy and can't settle to anything; I just have to get out. My diary is full of such occasions. On those all-too-rare calm winter days I work in the open at one of my favourite spots – the river, canal, or beach, perhaps, but usually my problem is finding a vantage point that is both sheltered from the biting wind and that has inspiring subjects for me to paint. Working from the car is one option I occasionally resort to. True, it can make a useful mobile hide if suitable subjects are near the road, but I have never found it entirely satisfactory; it's just too cramped. Instead, I often head for Rye Harbour Nature Reserve where I can usually find what I want, eventually.

Extract from my diary for 20th December, 11.00–16.30.

"*Very bright all day but with a chilly north-west wind increasing in strength throughout the day and only dropping at sunset. I start drawing Skylarks that are feeding around the edge of the Wader Pool. There are Snipe too, but they are keeping a very low profile until a Kestrel sends a dozen zigzagging skywards with rasping calls. The Skylarks take flight too, so I move to the Narrow Pits. Here I take refuge behind an oil tank, but there is no sign of yesterday's Dartford Warbler, and the Pochard, Tufted Duck and grebes are too distant, sheltering in the lee of the far bank.*

Finally, to Parkes Hide at the eastern end of Ternery Pool, where there are Mallard and Teal drakes in splendid plumage to watch and draw in reasonable comfort and close-up. Better still, a Water Rail is working round the edge of the pool just below the hide. It probes in the muddy margins and sometimes up-ends, duck-like, in the grey ooze. Teals seem to dislike Water Rails and make a lunge at any that pass too close. At dusk another Water Rail appears and a chase ensues. Two Little Grebes, plumage fluffed up like balls of fur, bob among the reeds."

Pett Pool 9·3·92   Robert R. Greenhalf

10·00 – 14·30 Hrs

Starlock 25·11·93 Looking towards Rye. Calm bright, misty start to day
Cloud moving in later with a light wind. Mild after several days of freezing temperatures.

Heron resting & preening on N.R.A. slip-way in middle ground, right side of picture.

Grey Wagtail & Kingfisher both perch briefly on lock. Heron later fishes, another one further down stream

Redshanks feed energetically on falling tide. Much noise & commotion from Rooks in nearby nesting trees.

Little Owl sitting motionless on low dead branch of oak near stream.

14th December '94   Wader-Pool Rye Harbour   11·00 - 16·00

Beautiful bright sunny day with a cold N. wind. Forty or more Snipe mostly
resting in dead rush & reed stems, a few feeding at the edge never far from
cover. In the bright light they are pale ochre with purple blue shadows. A few
Redshanks feed further out in the pool. Skylarks, never in one spot for long, feed
amongst the salicornia closer to the hide, frequently rising in a whorl to resettle again
in a new patch. The Snipe & Redshanks suddenly flatten themselves, melting into the
rushes as a Peregrine sweeps the pool.

19th December '94   Rye Harbour   14.00 - 16.30
Bright & cold, but the sun warm on my back as I paint
the view looking N.E. The reeds glow in the late afternoon
sun. A pair of Stonechats search for food amongst bulldozed
scrub near Rye Harbour village. A harsh scolding whitethroat
-like call proved to be a Dartford Warbler.

3rd January '95
Iden Lock
late afternoon

Sunny but cold, no wind. Heavy frost overnight has put a layer of ice on the canal, except for a few yards above the lock where water movement has kept it open. A kingfisher hunts from an overhanging bush.

102

9th December '94 Romney House
Early morning. Frost has set right after
a day of continuous heavy rain has flooded
fields below house. Bullfinches active in garden.

103

Time and tide

For me, as a painter of birds, there is no location as inspiring and challenging as the beach. I am captivated by the light and colours, particularly in the evening light, the patterns of mud and water, and above all by the birds.

There is a wild unapproachability to Curlews that I find an irresistible challenge, an aloofness which is summed up in that most wonderful of all cries that never fails to thrill me. Boldly-patterned black and white Oystercatchers are a gift to the painter, and so are those magnificent, huge Great Black-backed Gulls that sit statuesquely at the tideline, almost becoming a part of the rocks from which they morosely survey the shore. They make a perfect foil around which to compose the smaller more active avian elements of the beach scene: the Redshanks, Dunlins, Sanderlings, Ringed and Grey Plovers, and Turnstones.

The problems and frustrations of painting on the beach are many – not least of which is disturbance by people, dogs and low-flying aircraft, all of which can be expected, especially in summer. The evenings, though, are often surprisingly quiet and calm and the colours magnificent, heightened by the low orange light, but time is strictly limited and the air is often too damp for the paint to dry. This can sometimes lend a beautiful luminosity to the watercolour that is difficult to achieve in any other way, but it makes finishing a picture in one go an impossibility.

The tide rules here: if it comes in, sweeping away your subject before you have finished, then there is nothing to be done but to pack up and pray for similar conditions the next day. But in spite of these inherent difficulties, I find great exhilaration in painting on a rising tide. The impending deadline sharpens the senses wonderfully; decisions are split-second and you have to paint intuitively – it's a make or break strategy. The Pett Level shoreline is my favourite venue on a flowing tide. The rising water pushes the birds towards me, concentrating them on the last remaining rocks whilst the breaking waves provide a dramatic backdrop. As they finally rise, calling, before the on-rushing waves, and pass overhead to the fields, the Curlews and Oystercatchers are a splendid sight, and if time and tide defeat me there are always the Turnstones still busy probing the tideline, just asking to be drawn.

Robert R. Greenhalf

Portland 5.2.94   Robert K. Greenleaf

Wild swans and marsh skies

Today the sky is beautiful for painting; the clouds, tinged pink and ochre with purple-blue shadows, recede in ranks to the horizon where they merge into a blue haze. The water in the dykes is a deep ultramarine-purple to a rich red-brown at my feet. The sun, between clouds, is bright, clear and intense, bleaching the reeds almost to white, lighting to an intense orange the tops of willow trees on a distant bank, and casting the darkest of shadows on the fields and trees.

A Peregrine appears beneath a whirl of scattering Lapwings, Golden Plovers, Dunlins and Snipe. It passes quite close to me, moving apparently without effort into the strong wind. The heavy torpedo body never fails to impress me – it is a powerful fighter-plane of a bird. A Kestrel I see soon after looks frail and delicate by comparison; buffeted by the wind it seeks the lee of the bank for shelter.

At two o'clock, as I finish the painting, it suddenly gets colder. My hands, which up to now have felt quite warm, are very cold and further work would be difficult. A brisk walk back to the car does little to improve things. The wind has a real bite to it and I decide that the rest of the day's work will have to be done from the car.

I drive a few miles along winding marsh lanes that top the old inning walls, and find the Bewick's Swan flock on a winter wheat field, close to where it was yesterday. It is sunny now and the swans are backlit with a rim of warm white on top and the rest of their bodies in a shadow of the most beautiful pale blue. In the field behind there are sheep with Lapwings, Golden Plovers and Starlings feeding amongst them. The land-scape recedes in a series of verticals like stage scenery. Behind the sheep, a line of reed heads are like white torches against a grey-green bank and finally, in a haze, the blue-grey of the old cliff-line forms a backdrop.

I draw and paint feverishly to capture the scene, but the sun disappears behind a wall of cloud that rose to meet it above the cliff-line, and the colours all change. The swans become white again with subtle blue-grey shadows beneath, tinged with a yellow-green reflecting up from the field. There is less contrast, more detail in the distant cliff, the 'wobbly' haze has gone and, curiously, the wheat in front of the swans has turned almost to lemon yellow in the afterglow.

A Barn Owl hunts along the road bank, Grey Partridges call from the wheat, and half a dozen Moorhens have materialised on the edge of the field. The swans become more excited as the light fades. There is not much feeding going on now; most birds are walking around with heads held high and with much bobbing and calling. A few birds take off, heading for the flood where they roost. They run and flap to get airborne. The wind has died away and there are lightning flashes over the channel, but no sound of thunder. Another group of swans leaves, then another. Soon afterwards the remainder follow and I head for home.

3rd March '95 Mid afternoon, Romney Marsh. 140 Bewick's Swans feeding on Winter wheat,
large flocks of Lapwings, Golden Plovers & Starlings feeding amongst sheep in field behind.

Robert R. Greenhalf
Castle Water 16·1·97

9th March '95 Romney Marsh

Mainly sunny with an
odd shower, fresh S. wind.
Nine Bewick's Swans fly in
from a neighbouring wheat field
to drink & bathe.

Several Black-headed Gulls
feeding over the flood are in
summer plumage. A Peregrine
perched on a molehill on the
far side causes little attention
apart from a mobbing Lapwing,
but as soon as it takes to
the wing, pandemonium breaks
out.

As I shelter from a shower in
a hut, I find I am sharing it
with a hunting weasel.

Holton 2.3.94   Robert R. Greenhalf.

Norfolk geese

Visit the North Norfolk coast in winter and you cannot fail to be aware of the geese – they are there in their thousands. Densely packed flocks of Brent Geese surge like a black tide across the coastal grazing marshes, a thousand beaks cropping in unison. Murmurings rise to a clamour as they lift off to pastures new or out onto the mudflats – a sight that cannot fail to impress. Pinkfeet can be more elusive as they range over a wider area, often gleaning the newly harvested potato fields far inland, However, at Holkham they seem to favour the rough pasture fields to the landward side of the pine-clad coastal dunes.

On the 2nd March I found them without much effort:

> *"Half a mile along the path that winds along the base of the dunes, I catch my first glimpse of the grey mass of geese a little ahead of me. Eager not to miss the chance, I begin to draw, aiming the 'scope between the tree trunks. But it is cold here, there is a bitter wind and the trees are keeping the warmth of the sun from me. Ten minutes is enough, there must be a better vantage point.*
>
> *A few hundred yards further on the track changes direction, there is shelter from the wind and I am in the sun. The geese are closer, too. I walk slowly and carefully now, no quick movements, until I find a gateway with a clear view of the geese and even a bank to sit on. Gingerly I adjust my tripod and 'scope and get my paper and paints ready. The geese seem not unduly worried, no doubt they are used to people walking the track and stopping to observe them.*
>
> *Unlike the tightly-packed Brent Geese flocks that seem to move as one, the Pinkfeet are more spread out, scattered across the field in loose groups, more relaxed and less ordered. Two splendid cock Pheasants are explosions of bronze and gold in an otherwise subdued palette of predominantly ochre grass, subtle purple-grey and brown geese, and hazy purple-brown of ploughed earth and distant hawthorn break.*
>
> *The painting finished, there is still a little light left for exploring further along the track. I come across a hide with views across a reed-fringed pool to more meadows, and the sun setting over low, rolling Norfolk hills. The last orange rays catch a couple of cock Pheasants sparring close to the hide – an irresistible subject with which to close the day. As I walk back in the gathering dusk, the geese are heading off along the coast to roost on some distant sandbank."*

28·2·94   CLEY EYE

Bright at first but cloudy by
11 & a little light rain by 1 p.m.
Fairly mild but chilly wind from
on-shore. Many breats coming
low over the car park from
Blakeney Harbour
& landing on the
Reserve.

Walked along
beach towards
Blakeney Point.
Masses of Brents
resting on mud

groups of 40 or 50
breaking off & heading for Cley every few
minutes. When I got back
to the car there was a

huge flock of Brents only
2 or 300 yds away. Worked out
a composition with Brents & Black headed &
Common Gulls which were associating. Finished
painting as the light disappeared at 17·30.

Tremendous noise when
the flock of maybe 2 or 3 thousand
Brents take to the air - wing beats
like thunder of a distant explosion
accompanied by a thousand 'yelps'.

Many distant wigeon visible
only when put up by planes. Also
20-30 Avocets & 20 Whitefronts.

120

Winter windows

Winter solstice, 21st December: relentless rain and gloom. By eight o'clock there was only half-light and now, at ten, we still need the lights switched on. Outside the only movement is of raindrops, the only sounds an assortment of dull plops and bass drumming as the rain falls into puddles, onto leaves, corrugated iron, water butts and dustbin lids, or trickles down roofs, gutters and pipes. Inside, Sally practices Latin rhythms on her bongos, echoing the tattoo of raindrops.

Two days ago a male Blackcap moved silently through the branches of our pear tree. I glimpsed it from the kitchen window as I waited for the kettle to boil. It was only visible for a minute, then it was gone, off along the hedgerow and out of sight. Views from windows are nearly always like this, brief, but often memorable.

One day in November last year, a female Sparrowhawk suddenly alighted on a branch of the ash tree, only three or four yards from my studio window. She balanced awkwardly on one long, yellow leg. From the other dangled a limp male Blackbird, crimson and jet. We stared, each paralysed by surprise, each aware of the other but neither daring to move for perhaps thirty seconds before she broke the spell and flew off heavily. Throughout December and into January, for as long as the berries last, flocks of shy Redwings and Fieldfares, like storm-tossed leaves, descend on the Holly and Hawthorn bushes in our front hedge. Restless and impulsive, they ravish the berries for a few minutes, then are off in a whirl across the field – perpetual wanderers.

I have a bird table in front of one of my studio windows so that I can watch as I print my etchings – a tedious and repetitive task. It comes into its own during really cold weather, such as 6th December this year:

"Printing Christmas cards, Vanessa and I kept an eye on the comings and goings at the bird table. Starlings, magnificent in their white-spotted winter plumage, were puffed up against the cold like balloons with sharp projections fore and aft for beak, wings and tail, and feet barely visible. When the Starlings weren't monopolising it a crowd of sparrows took over. Even the Robin, who usually clears the table, was intimidated by their number and was reduced to snatching the odd scrap from the edge and retreating to the ground with it. Odd Chaffinches joined the sparrows and in the occasional lulls in activity a Dunnock would quietly feed. But all, even the Starlings, were swept away by the surprise raids of a Magpie.

Suddenly, a Great Spotted Woodpecker that had earlier enlivened our coffee break by visiting the nut-feeder on the veranda, landed on a small oak tree behind the table. For a few minutes it hammered at the rather unpromising, smooth-looking bark before disappearing."

Two winters ago, snow in February that lay for a week brought a Woodcock to our garden. It spent several days with us, burrowing into the snow to probe the leaf litter beneath with its long beak, often only a few feet from where I sat in the studio painting its richly patterned plumage of warm ochres, browns and greys, which were so beautifully set off by the cool blue shadows of the snow. For once I had a subject that was co-operative.

122

Woodland View, N. Walsham

4·3·94

4 ♂♂ & 1 ♀ Bramblings
coming to bird table
Much variation in
head pattern of ♂♂
Some almost solid black, others very little

♂ Siskin on Nut feeder

Chaffinches

2nd February '95 Romney House
From the Studio window. Bright, frosty
morning. Many birds visiting bird table –
many House Sparrows & Greenfinches. Most surprised
when a cock Pheasant flew in & began to feed beneath table!

23·3·94   Romney House
Blue, Great & occasional Long tailed Tits
on peanuts feeder & Shoulder bone
of Lamb.

4th February '75
Ronney House - Frosty.
Magpies feeding with
Sheep.